The Vibrant Vegetarian

Creative and Sustainable Vegetarian Cookbook

Harper Isley

Copyright © 2023 - All rights reserved.

The content contained within this book may not be reproduced, duplicated,or transmitted without direct written permission from the author or the publisher.

Under no circumstances will any blame or legal responsibility be held againstthe publisher, or author, for any damages, reparation, or monetary loss due to the information contained within this book. Either directly or indirectly.

Legal Notice: This book is copyright protected. This book is only for personal use. You cannot amend, distribute, sell, use, quote, or paraphrase any part, or the content within this book, without the consent of the author or publisher.

Disclaimer Notice: Please note the information contained within this document is for educational and entertainment purposes only. All effort has been executed topresent accurate, up-to-date, and reliable, complete information. No warranties of any kind are declared or implied. Readers acknowledge that theauthor is not engaging in the rendering of legal, financial, medical, orprofessional advice. The content within this book has been derived from various sources. Please consult a licensed professional before attempting anytechniques outlined in this book.

By reading this document, the reader agrees that under no circumstances is the author responsible for any losses, direct or indirect, which are incurred asa result of the use of the information contained within this document, including, but not limited to, — errors, omissions, or inaccuracies.

Table of the Contents

Breakfast

Overnight Oats

Ingredients:

- 1/2 cup rolled oats
- 1/2 cup milk (or plant-based milk)
- 1/4 cup Greek yogurt (or plant-based yogurt)
- 1/2 banana, mashed
- 1 tbsp chia seeds
- 1 tbsp honey (or maple syrup)
- 1/2 tsp vanilla extract

Instructions:

1. In a mason jar or bowl, mix together oats, milk, yogurt, banana, chia seeds, honey, and vanilla extract.
2. Cover and refrigerate overnight.
3. In the morning, add toppings of your choice, such as fresh berries, sliced banana, nuts, or granola.

Avocado Toast

Ingredients:

- 1 slice of whole grain bread
- 1/2 ripe avocado, mashed
- Salt and pepper to taste
- Optional toppings: sliced tomato, sprouts, sliced radish, everything bagel seasoning

Instructions:

1. Toast bread until golden brown.
2. Spread mashed avocado on top of toast.
3. Sprinkle with salt and pepper.
4. Add any additional toppings of your choice.

Veggie Breakfast Burrito

Ingredients:

- 1 whole wheat tortilla
- 2 eggs, scrambled
- 1/4 cup black beans, rinsed and drained
- 1/4 cup diced tomatoes
- 1/4 cup diced bell peppers

- 2 tbsp shredded cheese
- Salsa or hot sauce, for serving

Instructions:

1. In a skillet over medium heat, cook scrambled eggs until set.
2. Add black beans, tomatoes, and bell peppers to the skillet and cook until vegetables are tender.
3. Warm tortilla in the microwave for 10 seconds.
4. Spread egg and vegetable mixture onto tortilla and sprinkle with cheese.
5. Roll up burrito and serve with salsa or hot sauce.

Banana Pancakes

Ingredients:

- 1 ripe banana, mashed
- 1 egg
- 1/4 cup whole wheat flour
- 1/4 cup milk (or plant-based milk)
- 1 tsp baking powder
- 1/4 tsp cinnamon
- 1/4 tsp vanilla extract
- Butter or oil, for cooking

Instructions:

1. In a bowl, whisk together mashed banana and egg until smooth.
2. Add flour, milk, baking powder, cinnamon, and vanilla extract. Mix until well combined.
3. Heat a skillet over medium heat and add a small amount of butter or oil.
4. Pour 1/4 cup batter onto skillet and cook until bubbles form on the surface, then flip and cook until golden brown on both sides.
5. Repeat with remaining batter.

Yogurt Parfait

Ingredients:

- 1 cup Greek yogurt (or plant-based yogurt)
- 1/2 cup mixed fresh berries (such as strawberries, blueberries, and raspberries)
- 1/4 cup granola
- 1 tbsp honey

Instructions:

1. In a jar or bowl, layer yogurt, berries, and granola.
2. Drizzle honey over the top.
3. Repeat layers until all ingredients are used up.

4. Serve immediately.

Tofu Scramble

Ingredients:

- 1 block extra-firm tofu
- 1/4 cup diced onion
- 1/4 cup diced bell peppers
- 1/2 tsp garlic powder
- 1/2 tsp turmeric
- Salt and pepper to taste
- 1 tbsp olive oil

Instructions:

1. Drain and crumble tofu into a bowl.
2. In a skillet over medium heat, sauté onion and bell peppers in olive oil until tender.
3. Add crumbled tofu, garlic powder, turmeric, salt, and pepper. Cook until tofu is heated through and lightly browned.
4. Serve hot with toast or on a tortilla with salsa.

Sweet Potato and Black Bean Hash

Ingredients:

- 1 medium sweet potato, peeled and diced
- 1/2 cup black beans, rinsed and drained
- 1/4 cup diced onion
- 1/4 cup diced bell pepper
- 1 tsp chili powder
- Salt and pepper to taste
- 1 tbsp olive oil
- 1-2 eggs (optional)

Instructions:

1. In a skillet over medium heat, sauté sweet potato, black beans, onion, and bell pepper in olive oil until sweet potato is tender.
2. Add chili powder, salt, and pepper. Cook for an additional 1-2 minutes.
3. Serve hot with a fried or scrambled egg on top, if desired.

Strawberry Chia Jam

Ingredients:

- 2 cups sliced fresh strawberries
- 2 tbsp chia seeds
- 1 tbsp honey (or maple syrup)

Instructions:

1. In a blender or food processor, puree strawberries until smooth.
2. Pour puree into a bowl and stir in chia seeds and honey.
3. Cover and refrigerate for at least 30 minutes, until mixture thickens and becomes jam-like in texture.
4. Serve on toast, yogurt, or oatmeal.

Baked Eggs in Tomato Cups

Ingredients:

- 2 medium tomatoes
- 2 eggs
- Salt and pepper to taste
- 1 tbsp chopped fresh herbs (such as parsley or basil)

Instructions:

1. Preheat oven to 375°F (190°C).
2. Cut off the top of each tomato and scoop out the seeds and pulp with a spoon.
3. Crack an egg into each tomato cup.
4. Season with salt and pepper.
5. Place the tomatoes in a baking dish and bake for 20-25 minutes, until eggs are set to your liking.
6. Sprinkle with fresh herbs before serving.

Spinach and Feta Frittata

Ingredients:

- 4 large eggs
- 1/4 cup milk (or plant-based milk)
- 1/2 cup chopped fresh spinach
- 1/4 cup crumbled feta cheese
- 1/4 cup chopped onion
- Salt and pepper to taste
- 1 tbsp olive oil

Instructions:

1. Preheat oven to 375°F (190°C).
2. In a bowl, whisk together eggs and milk until well combined.

3. Stir in spinach, feta cheese, onion, salt, and pepper.
4. Heat olive oil in an oven-safe skillet over medium heat.
5. Pour egg mixture into skillet and cook for 2-3 minutes, until bottom is set.
6. Transfer skillet to oven and bake for 10-15 minutes, until top is set and lightly browned.
7. Slice into wedges and serve hot.

Apple Cinnamon Baked Oatmeal

Ingredients:

- 2 cups old-fashioned oats
- 2 cups milk (or plant-based milk)
- 1 apple, peeled and chopped
- 1/4 cup chopped nuts (such as pecans or almonds)
- 1/4 cup maple syrup
- 1 tsp cinnamon
- 1/4 tsp salt
- Butter or oil, for greasing the baking dish

Instructions:

1. Preheat oven to 375°F (190°C).
2. In a bowl, mix together oats, milk, apple, nuts, maple syrup, cinnamon, and salt.

3. Grease a baking dish with butter or oil.
4. Pour oat mixture into the baking dish and spread evenly.
5. Bake for 35-40 minutes, until the top is golden brown and the oatmeal is set.
6. Serve hot with additional milk and/or maple syrup, if desired.

Mediterranean Breakfast Pita

Ingredients:

- 1 whole wheat pita bread
- 1/4 cup hummus
- 1/4 cup chopped cucumber
- 1/4 cup chopped tomato
- 1/4 cup crumbled feta cheese
- 1 tbsp chopped fresh parsley
- Salt and pepper to taste

Instructions:

1. Slice the pita bread in half to create two pockets.
2. Spread hummus evenly inside each pocket.
3. Stuff each pocket with chopped cucumber, chopped tomato, and crumbled feta cheese.
4. Season with salt and pepper and sprinkle with fresh parsley.
5. Serve immediately.

Shakshuka

Ingredients:

- 1 tbsp olive oil
- 1/2 onion, diced
- 1 red bell pepper, diced
- 3 cloves garlic, minced
- 1 tsp ground cumin
- 1 tsp paprika
- 1/4 tsp cayenne pepper (optional)
- 1 can (14 oz) diced tomatoes
- Salt and pepper to taste
- 4 large eggs
- Feta cheese, crumbled
- Fresh parsley, chopped

Instructions:

1. Heat olive oil in a large skillet over medium heat.
2. Add onion and bell pepper and sauté until softened, about 5 minutes.
3. Add garlic, cumin, paprika, and cayenne pepper (if using) and sauté for another minute.
4. Pour in diced tomatoes and their juices, and season with salt and pepper.
5. Simmer for 10-15 minutes, until the sauce has thickened.
6. Use a spoon to create 4 wells in the sauce.

7. Crack an egg into each well.
8. Cover the skillet and cook until the eggs are set to your liking, about 5-7 minutes.
9. Sprinkle with crumbled feta cheese and chopped parsley.
10. Serve hot with crusty bread.

Vegan Tofu Breakfast Sandwich

Ingredients:

- 4 slices of bread
- 1 block of firm tofu, drained and pressed
- 1 tbsp nutritional yeast
- 1/4 tsp garlic powder
- 1/4 tsp onion powder
- Salt and pepper to taste
- 1/2 avocado, mashed
- 1 tbsp lemon juice
- 4 slices of tomato
- Baby spinach leaves

Instructions:

1. Toast bread slices.
2. In a bowl, crumble tofu and mix in nutritional yeast, garlic powder, onion powder, salt, and pepper.

3. Heat a skillet over medium-high heat and add the tofu mixture.
4. Cook for 5-7 minutes, until the tofu is browned and crispy.
5. In a small bowl, mix mashed avocado and lemon juice.
6. Spread avocado mixture on one slice of bread.
7. Top with tomato slices, spinach leaves, and the cooked tofu.
8. Place another slice of bread on top.
9. Serve hot.

Blueberry Chia Seed Pudding

Ingredients:

- 1 cup unsweetened almond milk (or any milk of your choice)
- 1/4 cup chia seeds
- 1/4 tsp vanilla extract
- 1 tbsp maple syrup
- 1/2 cup fresh blueberries
- 1 tbsp sliced almonds

Instructions:

1. In a jar or container with a lid, mix together almond milk, chia seeds, vanilla extract, and maple syrup.
2. Stir in fresh blueberries.
3. Cover and refrigerate for at least 2 hours, or overnight.
4. To serve, sprinkle with sliced almonds.

Vegan Banana Bread

Ingredients:

- 3 ripe bananas, mashed
- 1/3 cup vegetable oil
- 1/2 cup brown sugar
- 2 cups all-purpose flour
- 1 tsp baking powder
- 1 tsp baking soda
- 1/2 tsp salt
- 1 tsp cinnamon
- 1/2 cup chopped walnuts (optional)

Instructions:

1. Preheat oven to 350°F (175°C).
2. In a mixing bowl, combine mashed bananas, vegetable oil, and brown sugar.

3. In a separate bowl, whisk together flour, baking powder, baking soda, salt, and cinnamon.
4. Add dry ingredients to wet ingredients and mix until just combined.
5. Stir in chopped walnuts (if using).
6. Pour batter into a greased loaf pan.
7. Bake for 50-60 minutes, or until a toothpick inserted into the center comes out clean.
8. Let cool for 10 minutes before slicing.

Vegan Tofu and Veggie Breakfast Bowl

Ingredients:

- 1 block of firm tofu, drained and pressed
- 1 tbsp olive oil
- 1/2 red bell pepper, sliced
- 1/2 yellow bell pepper, sliced
- 1/2 onion, sliced
- 1 garlic clove, minced
- 1 tsp paprika
- Salt and pepper to taste
- Baby spinach leaves
- Cherry tomatoes, halved
- Avocado slices
- Hot sauce (optional)

Instructions:

1. In a large skillet, heat olive oil over medium-high heat.
2. Add sliced bell peppers, onion, and garlic, and sauté until softened, about 5 minutes.
3. Crumble tofu into the skillet and stir in paprika, salt, and pepper.
4. Cook for 5-7 minutes, until tofu is browned and crispy.
5. Divide baby spinach leaves into serving bowls.
6. Top with the tofu and veggie mixture, cherry tomatoes, and avocado slices.
7. Drizzle with hot sauce (if using).
8. Serve hot.

Vegan Chocolate Chip Pancakes

Ingredients:

- 2 cups all-purpose flour
- 2 tbsp granulated sugar
- 1 tbsp baking powder
- 1/2 tsp salt
- 2 cups almond milk (or any milk of your choice)
- 1/4 cup vegetable oil
- 1 tsp vanilla extract
- 1/2 cup vegan chocolate chips

Instructions:

1. In a mixing bowl, whisk together flour, sugar, baking powder, and salt.
2. In a separate bowl, combine almond milk, vegetable oil, and vanilla extract.
3. Add wet ingredients to dry ingredients and mix until just combined.
4. Stir in vegan chocolate chips.
5. Heat a non-stick griddle or skillet over medium-high heat.
6. Pour 1/4 cup of batter for each pancake onto the griddle or skillet.
7. Cook until bubbles appear on the surface, then flip and cook until lightly browned.
8. Serve hot with maple syrup and fresh fruit.

Green Smoothie Bowl

Ingredients:

- 1 cup frozen mixed berries
- 1 banana
- 1 cup spinach
- 1/2 cup almond milk
- 1 tbsp honey

- 1 tbsp chia seeds
- Toppings: fresh berries, granola, shredded coconut, sliced almonds

Instructions:

1. Add the frozen berries, banana, spinach, almond milk, honey, and chia seeds to a blender.
2. Blend until smooth and creamy, adding more almond milk as needed to reach your desired consistency.
3. Pour the smoothie into a bowl and add your desired toppings.

Mushroom and Spinach Quiche

Ingredients:

- 1 pie crust
- 1 tbsp olive oil
- 1/2 onion, chopped
- 1 cup mushrooms, sliced
- 2 cups spinach
- 4 eggs
- 1/2 cup milk
- 1/2 cup shredded cheese
- Salt and pepper to taste

Instructions:

1. Preheat oven to 375°F (190°C).
2. Heat the olive oil in a skillet over medium heat. Add the onion and mushrooms and sauté until softened, about 5 minutes. Add the spinach and cook until wilted, about 2 minutes.
3. Beat the eggs and milk together in a bowl. Stir in the cheese, salt, and pepper.
4. Place the pie crust in a 9-inch pie dish. Pour the mushroom and spinach mixture into the crust. Pour the egg mixture over the top.
5. Bake for 35-40 minutes or until the quiche is set and golden brown.

Cinnamon Roll Waffles

Ingredients:

- 2 cups flour
- 2 tbsp sugar
- 2 tsp baking powder
- 1/2 tsp baking soda
- 1/2 tsp salt
- 2 cups milk
- 2 eggs

- 1/4 cup vegetable oil
- 1 tsp vanilla extract
- 1/2 cup brown sugar
- 1 tbsp cinnamon
- Cream cheese glaze: 2 oz cream cheese, 1/2 cup powdered sugar, 1 tsp vanilla extract, 2 tbsp milk

Instructions:

1. Preheat waffle iron.
2. In a large bowl, whisk together the flour, sugar, baking powder, baking soda, and salt.
3. In a separate bowl, whisk together the milk, eggs, vegetable oil, and vanilla extract.
4. Pour the wet ingredients into the dry ingredients and stir until just combined.
5. In a small bowl, mix together the brown sugar and cinnamon.
6. Pour the batter into the waffle iron, and sprinkle the cinnamon sugar mixture on top.
7. Close the waffle iron and cook for 4-5 minutes, or until golden brown.
8. To make the cream cheese glaze, beat together the cream cheese, powdered sugar, vanilla extract, and milk until smooth.
9. Drizzle the glaze over the warm waffles and serve immediately.

Chickpea Flour Pancakes

Ingredients:

- 1 cup chickpea flour
- 1/4 tsp salt
- 1/4 tsp ground turmeric
- 1/4 tsp baking powder
- 1/2 cup water
- 2 tbsp olive oil
- Optional toppings: avocado, tomatoes, greens, hot sauce

Instructions:

1. In a medium bowl, whisk together chickpea flour, salt, turmeric, and baking powder.
2. Slowly add in water and olive oil, whisking until a smooth batter forms.
3. Heat a nonstick skillet over medium heat and pour in 1/4 cup batter for each pancake.
4. Cook for 2-3 minutes on each side, or until golden brown.
5. Serve with your favorite toppings.

Vegan Breakfast Sausage Patties

Ingredients:

- 1 cup cooked lentils
- 1/2 cup rolled oats
- 1/4 cup chopped onion
- 1 tbsp ground flaxseed
- 1 tbsp nutritional yeast
- 1 tsp dried sage
- 1/2 tsp garlic powder
- 1/2 tsp smoked paprika
- Salt and pepper to taste
- 1 tbsp olive oil

Instructions:

1. In a food processor, pulse together cooked lentils, rolled oats, onion, flaxseed, nutritional yeast, sage, garlic powder, smoked paprika, salt, and pepper until well combined.
2. Form the mixture into 8 patties.
3. Heat olive oil in a nonstick skillet over medium heat and cook patties for 3-4 minutes on each side, or until crispy and browned.
4. Serve with your favorite breakfast sides.

Vegan Breakfast Tacos

Ingredients:

- 8 corn tortillas
- 1 can black beans, rinsed and drained
- 1/2 cup diced bell pepper
- 1/2 cup diced onion
- 1/2 tsp chili powder
- 1/2 tsp cumin
- 1/4 tsp garlic powder
- Salt and pepper to taste
- Optional toppings: avocado, salsa, hot sauce, cilantro

Instructions:

1. Heat a nonstick skillet over medium heat and warm the corn tortillas.
2. In a separate skillet, sauté black beans, bell pepper, and onion until tender.
3. Stir in chili powder, cumin, garlic powder, salt, and pepper, and cook for an additional minute.
4. Divide the black bean mixture evenly among the tortillas and top with your desired toppings.
5. Serve and enjoy!

Vegan Breakfast Burrito Bowl

Ingredients:

- 1 cup cooked brown rice
- 1 can black beans, drained and rinsed
- 1 avocado, diced
- 1/2 red onion, diced
- 1/2 red bell pepper, diced
- 1/2 cup corn
- 1/4 cup cilantro, chopped
- 1 tbsp lime juice
- Salt and pepper to taste
- Salsa and hot sauce (optional)

Instructions:

1. In a bowl, combine the cooked rice, black beans, diced avocado, red onion, red bell pepper, corn, and cilantro.
2. Drizzle with lime juice and season with salt and pepper to taste.
3. Serve with salsa and hot sauce, if desired.

Vegan Breakfast Pizza

Ingredients:

- 1 pre-made pizza crust
- 1/4 cup pizza sauce
- 1/2 cup vegan shredded mozzarella cheese
- 1/2 red bell pepper, sliced
- 1/2 onion, sliced
- 1/4 cup sliced mushrooms
- 1/4 cup sliced black olives
- 1 tbsp olive oil
- Salt and pepper to taste

Instructions:

1. Preheat the oven to 425°F (220°C).
2. Spread the pizza sauce evenly over the pre-made crust.
3. Sprinkle the vegan shredded mozzarella cheese over the sauce.
4. Top with sliced red bell pepper, onion, mushrooms, and black olives.
5. Drizzle with olive oil and season with salt and pepper to taste.
6. Bake for 12-15 minutes or until the cheese is melted and the crust is crispy.

Tofu and Vegetable Breakfast Scramble

Ingredients:

- 1 block firm tofu
- 1 red bell pepper, chopped
- 1 yellow onion, chopped
- 1 garlic clove, minced
- 1 tbsp olive oil
- 1/2 tsp turmeric
- 1/4 tsp cumin
- 1/4 tsp paprika
- Salt and pepper, to taste

Instructions:

1. Heat the olive oil in a pan over medium heat. Add the chopped bell pepper and onion and sauté until softened, about 5-7 minutes.
2. Add the minced garlic and spices to the pan and sauté for another minute.
3. Crumble the tofu into the pan and mix everything together. Cook until the tofu is heated through and slightly browned, about 5-7 minutes.
4. Serve hot and enjoy!

Appetizers and Snacks

Caprese Skewers

Ingredients:

- Cherry tomatoes
- Fresh mozzarella balls
- Fresh basil leaves
- Balsamic glaze
- Salt and pepper to taste

Instructions:

1. Rinse the cherry tomatoes and basil leaves.
2. Cut the mozzarella balls in half.
3. Skewer a cherry tomato, a half piece of mozzarella, and a basil leaf onto each skewer.
4. Drizzle with balsamic glaze and sprinkle with salt and pepper to taste.
5. Serve and enjoy!

Sweet Potato Fries

Ingredients:

- 2 large sweet potatoes
- 2 tbsp. olive oil
- 1 tsp. smoked paprika
- 1 tsp. garlic powder
- Salt and pepper to taste

Instructions:

1. Preheat the oven to 400°F (200°C).
2. Cut the sweet potatoes into thin fries.
3. In a large bowl, toss the sweet potato fries with the olive oil, smoked paprika, garlic powder, salt, and pepper.
4. Spread the sweet potato fries in a single layer on a baking sheet.
5. Bake for 25-30 minutes or until crispy and browned.
6. Serve with your favorite dipping sauce and enjoy!

Guacamole

Ingredients:

- 2 ripe avocados
- 1 small onion, finely chopped
- 1 small tomato, diced
- 1 jalapeño, seeded and finely chopped
- Juice of 1 lime
- Salt and pepper to taste

Instructions:

1. Cut the avocados in half, remove the pits, and scoop out the flesh into a medium bowl.
2. Mash the avocado with a fork or potato masher until desired consistency is reached.
3. Add the chopped onion, diced tomato, jalapeño, lime juice, salt, and pepper to the bowl with the avocado and mix well.
4. Taste and adjust seasoning as necessary.
5. Serve with tortilla chips or vegetables and enjoy!

Roasted Chickpeas

Ingredients:

- 1 can chickpeas (15 ounces), drained and rinsed
- 1 tablespoon olive oil
- 1/2 teaspoon ground cumin
- 1/2 teaspoon smoked paprika
- 1/2 teaspoon garlic powder
- 1/4 teaspoon salt

Instructions:

1. Preheat the oven to 400°F (200°C).
2. Rinse and drain the chickpeas, then pat them dry with a paper towel.
3. In a bowl, toss the chickpeas with the olive oil, cumin, smoked paprika, garlic powder, and salt.
4. Spread the chickpeas on a baking sheet lined with parchment paper.
5. Roast for 25-30 minutes, stirring occasionally, until crispy and golden brown.
6. Serve warm or at room temperature.

Hummus with Crudité

Ingredients:

- 1 can chickpeas (15 ounces), drained and rinsed
- 1/4 cup tahini
- 1/4 cup lemon juice
- 2 garlic cloves, minced
- 1/4 teaspoon salt
- 1/4 teaspoon ground cumin
- 1/4 cup water
- Assorted vegetables, such as carrots, celery, bell peppers, and cucumbers

Instructions:

1. In a food processor, combine the chickpeas, tahini, lemon juice, garlic, salt, and cumin. Process until smooth.
2. With the food processor running, slowly add the water until the hummus is creamy and smooth.
3. Transfer the hummus to a serving bowl and chill in the refrigerator until ready to serve.
4. Wash and chop the vegetables into bite-sized pieces.
5. Arrange the vegetables on a platter and serve with the hummus.

Roasted Red Pepper and Feta Dip

Ingredients:

- 2 roasted red peppers, chopped
- 4 ounces feta cheese, crumbled
- 1/4 cup plain Greek yogurt
- 1 garlic clove, minced
- 1/4 teaspoon smoked paprika
- 1/4 teaspoon salt
- Fresh parsley, chopped, for garnish
- Pita chips or sliced vegetables, for serving

Instructions:

1. In a food processor, combine the roasted red peppers, feta cheese, Greek yogurt, garlic, smoked paprika, and salt. Process until smooth.
2. Transfer the dip to a serving bowl and garnish with chopped parsley.
3. Serve with pita chips or sliced vegetables.

Spinach and Artichoke Dip

Ingredients:

- 1 can (14 oz) artichoke hearts, drained and chopped
- 1 package (10 oz) frozen spinach, thawed and drained
- 1 cup grated Parmesan cheese
- 1 cup sour cream
- 1/2 cup mayonnaise
- 1 clove garlic, minced
- Salt and pepper to taste

Instructions:

1. Preheat oven to 375°F (190°C).
2. In a large bowl, mix together the chopped artichoke hearts, spinach, Parmesan cheese, sour cream, mayonnaise, and garlic.
3. Season with salt and pepper to taste.
4. Transfer the mixture to a baking dish and bake for 20-25 minutes, or until the top is golden brown and the dip is heated through.
5. Serve with crackers, pita chips, or fresh veggies.

Caponata

Ingredients:

- 1 large eggplant, diced
- 1 can (14 oz) diced tomatoes
- 1/2 cup chopped onion
- 1/2 cup chopped celery
- 1/2 cup chopped bell pepper
- 1/4 cup chopped kalamata olives
- 2 tablespoons capers
- 2 tablespoons red wine vinegar
- 2 tablespoons olive oil
- Salt and pepper to taste

Instructions:

1. Heat the olive oil in a large skillet over medium heat.
2. Add the diced eggplant and sauté for 5-7 minutes, or until tender.
3. Add the diced tomatoes, onion, celery, bell pepper, olives, capers, and red wine vinegar to the skillet.
4. Season with salt and pepper to taste.
5. Reduce the heat to low and let the mixture simmer for 15-20 minutes, or until the vegetables are soft and the flavors have melded together.
6. Serve the caponata warm or at room temperature with crostini or crackers.

Roasted Veggie Skewers

Ingredients:

- 1 zucchini, cut into rounds
- 1 yellow squash, cut into rounds
- 1 red onion, cut into chunks
- 1 red bell pepper, cut into chunks
- 1 green bell pepper, cut into chunks
- 1/4 cup olive oil
- 2 cloves garlic, minced
- 1 tablespoon balsamic vinegar
- 1 teaspoon dried oregano
- Salt and pepper to taste

Instructions:

1. Preheat oven to 425°F (220°C) and line a baking sheet with parchment paper.
2. In a large bowl, whisk together the olive oil, garlic, balsamic vinegar, oregano, salt, and pepper.
3. Add the zucchini, yellow squash, red onion, and bell peppers to the bowl and toss to coat.
4. Thread the vegetables onto skewers and place on the prepared baking sheet.
5. Roast for 20-25 minutes, or until the vegetables are tender and lightly browned.

6. Serve the skewers as a delicious and healthy snack or appetizer.

Stuffed Mushrooms

Ingredients:

- 16 large mushrooms, stems removed
- 1/2 cup breadcrumbs
- 1/2 cup grated parmesan cheese
- 1/4 cup chopped parsley
- 2 cloves garlic, minced
- 2 tbsp olive oil
- Salt and pepper to taste

Instructions:

1. Preheat the oven to 375°F (190°C).
2. In a bowl, combine the breadcrumbs, parmesan cheese, parsley, garlic, and olive oil. Mix well.
3. Season the mushroom caps with salt and pepper.
4. Stuff each mushroom cap with the breadcrumb mixture.
5. Arrange the stuffed mushrooms on a baking sheet and bake for 20-25 minutes, or until the mushrooms are tender and the stuffing is golden brown.

Crispy Zucchini Fritters

Ingredients:

- 2 medium zucchinis, grated
- 1/2 cup flour
- 1/4 cup grated parmesan cheese
- 1 egg
- 1 clove garlic, minced
- 2 tbsp chopped fresh parsley
- Salt and pepper to taste
- Olive oil for frying

Instructions:

1. In a bowl, combine the grated zucchini, flour, parmesan cheese, egg, garlic, parsley, salt, and pepper. Mix well.
2. Heat a thin layer of olive oil in a large skillet over medium-high heat.
3. Using a spoon, drop the zucchini mixture into the hot oil and flatten slightly to form a fritter.
4. Fry the fritters for 2-3 minutes on each side, or until golden brown and crispy.
5. Remove the fritters from the skillet and place them on paper towels to drain excess oil.
6. Serve warm with your favorite dipping sauce.

Baked Eggplant Chips

Ingredients:

- 1 large eggplant, sliced into thin rounds
- 1/2 cup breadcrumbs
- 1/4 cup grated parmesan cheese
- 1 tsp dried oregano
- Salt and pepper to taste
- Olive oil for brushing

Instructions:

1. Preheat the oven to 400°F (200°C).
2. In a bowl, combine the breadcrumbs, parmesan cheese, oregano, salt, and pepper. Mix well.
3. Brush the eggplant slices with olive oil on both sides.
4. Coat each slice with the breadcrumb mixture.
5. Arrange the eggplant slices in a single layer on a baking sheet lined with parchment paper.
6. Bake for 15-20 minutes, or until the eggplant is crispy and golden brown.
7. Serve warm with your favorite dipping sauce.

Creamy Avocado Dip

Ingredients:

- 2 ripe avocados, peeled and pitted
- 1/4 cup plain Greek yogurt
- 1/4 cup chopped fresh cilantro
- 1 clove garlic, minced
- Juice of 1 lime
- Salt and pepper to taste

Instructions:

1. In a bowl, mash the avocados with a fork.
2. Add the Greek yogurt, cilantro, garlic, lime juice, salt, and pepper. Mix well.
3. Adjust seasoning to taste.
4. Serve chilled with your favorite tortilla chips or vegetable sticks.

Tomato Bruschetta

Ingredients:

- 1 loaf French bread, sliced
- 6-8 ripe tomatoes, diced
- 3 cloves garlic, minced

- 1/4 cup fresh basil, chopped
- 1/4 cup extra virgin olive oil
- Salt and pepper to taste

Instructions:

1. Preheat the oven to 400°F.
2. Brush the bread slices with olive oil and place on a baking sheet.
3. Bake for 8-10 minutes, until toasted.
4. In a bowl, combine the diced tomatoes, garlic, basil, olive oil, salt, and pepper.
5. Spoon the tomato mixture over the toasted bread and serve.

Roasted Beet Hummus

Ingredients:

- 2 medium beets, roasted and chopped
- 1 can chickpeas, drained and rinsed
- 1/4 cup tahini
- 2 cloves garlic
- 1/4 cup lemon juice
- 1/4 cup olive oil

- Salt and pepper to taste

Instructions:

1. In a food processor, combine the roasted beets, chickpeas, tahini, garlic, lemon juice, and olive oil.
2. Process until smooth.
3. Season with salt and pepper to taste.
4. Serve with pita chips or veggies.

Cheesy Garlic Breadsticks

Ingredients:

- 1 pizza dough ball
- 1/4 cup unsalted butter, melted
- 2 cloves garlic, minced
- 1/2 cup mozzarella cheese, shredded
- 1/4 cup parmesan cheese, grated

Instructions:

1. Preheat the oven to 400°F.

2. Roll out the pizza dough on a floured surface and cut into breadsticks.
3. In a small bowl, mix together the melted butter and minced garlic.
4. Brush the garlic butter mixture over the breadsticks.
5. Top with shredded mozzarella and grated parmesan cheese.
6. Bake for 10-12 minutes, until the cheese is melted and the breadsticks are golden brown.

Spicy Roasted Chickpeas

Ingredients:

- 1 can chickpeas, drained and rinsed
- 1 tablespoon olive oil
- 1 teaspoon paprika
- 1/2 teaspoon cumin
- 1/2 teaspoon garlic powder
- 1/4 teaspoon cayenne pepper
- Salt to taste

Instructions:

1. Preheat the oven to 400°F.

2. In a bowl, mix together the chickpeas, olive oil, paprika, cumin, garlic powder, cayenne pepper, and salt.
3. Spread the chickpeas out in a single layer on a baking sheet.
4. Bake for 20-25 minutes, until crispy and golden brown.
5. Serve as a crunchy and spicy snack.

Vegan Buffalo Cauliflower Wings

Ingredients:

- 1 head of cauliflower
- 1/2 cup all-purpose flour
- 1/2 cup unsweetened almond milk
- 1 tsp garlic powder
- 1 tsp paprika
- 1/2 tsp salt
- 1/2 cup buffalo sauce

Instructions:

1. Preheat the oven to 450°F and line a baking sheet with parchment paper.
2. Cut the cauliflower into bite-sized pieces.

3. In a bowl, mix together the flour, almond milk, garlic powder, paprika, and salt until well combined.
4. Dip each cauliflower piece into the mixture, coating it well.
5. Place the coated cauliflower onto the prepared baking sheet and bake for 20 minutes, or until golden brown and crispy.
6. In a separate bowl, mix together the buffalo sauce and a tablespoon of melted vegan butter.
7. Once the cauliflower is done baking, toss it in the buffalo sauce mixture until evenly coated.
8. Serve hot with vegan ranch or blue cheese dressing.

Vegan Spinach and Artichoke Dip

Ingredients:

- 1 can (14 oz) artichoke hearts, drained and chopped
- 1 cup fresh spinach, chopped
- 1/2 cup vegan mayonnaise
- 1/2 cup vegan sour cream
- 1/2 cup nutritional yeast
- 2 cloves garlic, minced
- 1 tsp lemon juice
- Salt and pepper to taste

Instructions:

1. Preheat the oven to 350°F and grease a baking dish.
2. In a mixing bowl, combine the artichoke hearts, spinach, vegan mayonnaise, vegan sour cream, nutritional yeast, garlic, lemon juice, salt, and pepper.
3. Mix until well combined and transfer the mixture to the prepared baking dish.
4. Bake for 20-25 minutes, or until the top is golden brown and the dip is heated through.
5. Serve hot with tortilla chips or sliced baguette.

Vegan Baked Samosas

Ingredients:

- 2 large potatoes, peeled and diced
- 1/2 cup frozen green peas
- 1/2 cup chopped onion
- 2 cloves garlic, minced
- 1 tsp garam masala
- 1/2 tsp ground cumin
- 1/2 tsp ground coriander
- Salt and pepper to taste
- 12 sheets phyllo pastry
- 1/4 cup vegan butter, melted

Instructions:

1. Preheat the oven to 375°F and line a baking sheet with parchment paper.
2. In a saucepan, boil the diced potatoes until tender. Drain and set aside.
3. In a skillet, sauté the chopped onion and minced garlic until fragrant.
4. Add the cooked potatoes, frozen green peas, garam masala, ground cumin, ground coriander, salt, and pepper. Mix until well combined.
5. Cut the phyllo pastry into squares and place a spoonful of the potato mixture in the center of each square.
6. Fold the pastry over the filling to form a triangle and seal the edges with melted vegan butter.
7. Place the samosas onto the prepared baking sheet and bake for 20-25 minutes, or until golden brown.
8. Serve hot with chutney or dipping sauce.

Vegan Mushroom Pate

Ingredients:

- 2 cups chopped mushrooms
- 1/2 cup chopped onion
- 2 cloves garlic, minced

- 1/4 cup vegan butter
- 1/4 cup vegetable broth
- 1 tbsp soy sauce
- 1 tbsp nutritional yeast
- Salt and pepper to taste

Instructions:

1. In a skillet, sauté the chopped mushrooms, onion, and garlic in vegan butter until tender.
2. Add the vegetable broth, soy sauce, nutritional yeast, salt, and pepper to the skillet and cook for 10 minutes, or until most of the liquid has evaporated.
3. Transfer the mixture to a blender or food processor and blend until smooth.
4. Transfer the pate to a serving dish and chill in the refrigerator for at least an hour before serving.
5. Serve with crackers or bread.

Vegan Stuffed Grape Leaves

Ingredients:

- 1 jar grape leaves, drained and rinsed
- 1 cup cooked rice
- 1/2 cup chopped onion

- 2 cloves garlic, minced
- 1/2 cup chopped fresh parsley
- 1/4 cup chopped fresh mint
- 1/4 cup lemon juice
- Salt and pepper to taste

Instructions:

1. In a mixing bowl, combine the cooked rice, chopped onion, minced garlic, chopped parsley, chopped mint, lemon juice, salt, and pepper.
2. Take one grape leaf at a time and place a spoonful of the rice mixture in the center.
3. Fold the sides of the grape leaf over the filling, then roll up the leaf tightly.
4. Place the stuffed grape leaves in a baking dish and bake for 20-25 minutes, or until heated through.
5. Serve hot or cold with a dollop of vegan yogurt or tzatziki sauce.

Vegan Lentil Dip

Ingredients:

- 1 cup cooked lentils
- 1/2 cup chopped onion
- 2 cloves garlic, minced
- 1/4 cup tahini

- 1/4 cup lemon juice
- 1/4 cup vegetable broth
- 1 tsp ground cumin
- Salt and pepper to taste

Instructions:

1. In a food processor, blend the cooked lentils, chopped onion, minced garlic, tahini, lemon juice, vegetable broth, ground cumin, salt, and pepper until smooth.
2. Transfer the dip to a serving dish and chill in the refrigerator for at least an hour before serving.
3. Serve with pita chips or raw vegetables.

Vegan Spicy Edamame

Ingredients:

- 2 cups frozen edamame
- 1 tbsp olive oil
- 1 tbsp soy sauce
- 1 tsp chili powder
- 1/2 tsp garlic powder
- Salt and pepper to taste

Instructions:

1. Preheat the oven to 375°F and line a baking sheet with parchment paper.
2. In a mixing bowl, combine the frozen edamame, olive oil, soy sauce, chili powder, garlic powder, salt, and pepper.
3. Spread the mixture onto the prepared baking sheet and bake for 15-20 minutes, or until the edamame is heated through and slightly crispy.
4. Serve hot with a sprinkle of sesame seeds.

Vegan Nachos

Ingredients:

- 1 bag tortilla chips
- 1 cup black beans, drained and rinsed
- 1 cup corn kernels
- 1/2 cup diced tomato
- 1/2 cup diced red onion
- 1/2 cup sliced black olives
- 1/2 cup vegan cheddar cheese, shredded
- 1/4 cup chopped fresh cilantro
- 1 jalapeño pepper, thinly sliced

Instructions:

1. Preheat the oven to 375°F and line a baking sheet with parchment paper.
2. Arrange the tortilla chips in a single layer on the prepared baking sheet.
3. Sprinkle the black beans, corn kernels, diced tomato, diced red onion, sliced black olives, and vegan cheddar cheese over the tortilla chips.
4. Bake in the preheated oven for 10-15 minutes, or until the cheese is melted and bubbly.
5. Remove from the oven and sprinkle the chopped cilantro and sliced jalapeño pepper over the top.
6. Serve hot with salsa and guacamole on the side.

Vegan Spinach and Feta Pinwheels

Ingredients:

- 1 sheet puff pastry, thawed
- 1 cup frozen spinach, thawed and drained
- 1/2 cup vegan feta cheese, crumbled
- 1/4 cup chopped sun-dried tomatoes
- 1/4 cup chopped kalamata olives
- 1/4 cup chopped fresh parsley
- Salt and pepper to taste

Instructions:

1. Preheat the oven to 400°F and line a baking sheet with parchment paper.
2. Unfold the thawed puff pastry sheet onto a lightly floured surface.
3. Spread the thawed and drained spinach over the puff pastry sheet, leaving a 1-inch border around the edges.
4. Sprinkle the crumbled vegan feta cheese, chopped sun-dried tomatoes, chopped kalamata olives, chopped fresh parsley, salt, and pepper over the spinach.
5. Roll the puff pastry sheet up tightly from one end to the other, sealing the edges with a bit of water.
6. Cut the rolled-up pastry into 1-inch slices and place them on the prepared baking sheet.
7. Bake in the preheated oven for 15-20 minutes, or until golden brown and puffy.
8. Serve hot or at room temperature.

Vegan Bruschetta with White Bean Spread

Ingredients:

- 1 baguette, sliced
- 1 can white beans, drained and rinsed
- 1 clove garlic, minced
- 1 tbsp lemon juice
- 1 tbsp olive oil
- 1 tbsp chopped fresh basil

- Salt and pepper to taste

Instructions:

1. Preheat the oven to 375°F and line a baking sheet with parchment paper.
2. Arrange the baguette slices in a single layer on the prepared baking sheet.
3. In a food processor, blend the white beans, minced garlic, lemon juice, olive oil, chopped fresh basil, salt, and pepper until smooth.
4. Spread the white bean mixture over the baguette slices.
5. Bake in the preheated oven for 10-12 minutes, or until the bread is crispy and the topping is heated through.
6. Serve hot or at room temperature.

Soups

Creamy Carrot Soup

Ingredients:

- 6 large carrots, peeled and chopped
- 1 onion, chopped
- 4 cups vegetable broth
- 1/2 cup heavy cream
- Salt and pepper to taste
- Chopped fresh parsley, for garnish

Instructions:

1. In a large pot, sauté the chopped onions in a tablespoon of olive oil until translucent.
2. Add the chopped carrots and vegetable broth to the pot, and bring to a boil. Reduce heat and let simmer for about 25 minutes or until the carrots are soft.
3. Use an immersion blender or transfer the soup to a blender to puree until smooth.
4. Return the pureed soup to the pot, add the heavy cream, and heat over low heat.
5. Season with salt and pepper to taste.
6. Serve hot, garnished with chopped fresh parsley.

Lentil and Vegetable Soup

Ingredients:

- 1 onion, chopped
- 2 garlic cloves, minced
- 2 cups chopped vegetables (such as carrots, celery, and zucchini)
- 1 cup dried lentils, rinsed and drained
- 4 cups vegetable broth
- 1 teaspoon dried thyme
- Salt and pepper to taste
- Chopped fresh parsley, for garnish

Instructions:

1. In a large pot, sauté the chopped onion and minced garlic in a tablespoon of olive oil until softened.
2. Add the chopped vegetables, dried lentils, vegetable broth, and dried thyme to the pot, and bring to a boil. Reduce heat and let simmer for about 25 minutes or until the lentils are soft.
3. Season with salt and pepper to taste.
4. Serve hot, garnished with chopped fresh parsley.

Roasted Tomato Soup

Ingredients:

- 2 pounds Roma tomatoes, halved
- 1 onion, chopped
- 3 garlic cloves, minced
- 4 cups vegetable broth
- 1 teaspoon dried oregano
- Salt and pepper to taste
- Chopped fresh basil, for garnish

Instructions:

1. Preheat the oven to 400°F.
2. Place the halved Roma tomatoes on a baking sheet lined with parchment paper, and drizzle with a tablespoon of olive oil. Roast for about 30 minutes or until the tomatoes are soft and slightly charred.
3. In a large pot, sauté the chopped onion and minced garlic in a tablespoon of olive oil until softened.
4. Add the roasted tomatoes, vegetable broth, and dried oregano to the pot, and bring to a boil. Reduce heat and let simmer for about 15 minutes.
5. Use an immersion blender or transfer the soup to a blender to puree until smooth.
6. Season with salt and pepper to taste.
7. Serve hot, garnished with chopped fresh basil.

Spicy Black Bean Soup

Ingredients:

- 2 cans black beans, drained and rinsed
- 1 onion, chopped
- 2 garlic cloves, minced
- 1 jalapeño pepper, seeded and minced
- 4 cups vegetable broth
- 1 teaspoon ground cumin
- 1/2 teaspoon smoked paprika
- Salt and pepper to taste
- Chopped fresh cilantro, for garnish

Instructions:

1. In a large pot, sauté the chopped onion, minced garlic, and minced jalapeño pepper in a tablespoon of olive oil until softened.
2. Add the drained black beans, vegetable broth, ground cumin, and smoked paprika to the pot, and bring to a boil. Reduce heat and let simmer for about 15 minutes.
3. Use an immersion blender or transfer the soup to a blender to puree until smooth.
4. Season with salt and pepper to taste.
5. Serve hot, garnished with chopped fresh cilantro.

Creamy Potato Leek Soup

Ingredients:

- 2 leeks, white and light green parts only, chopped
- 2 garlic cloves, minced
- 3 potatoes, peeled and chopped
- 4 cups vegetable broth
- 1/2 cup heavy cream
- Salt and pepper to taste
- Chopped fresh chives, for garnish

Instructions:

1. In a large pot, sauté the chopped leeks and minced garlic in a tablespoon of olive oil until softened.
2. Add the chopped potatoes and vegetable broth to the pot, and bring to a boil. Reduce heat and let simmer for about 25 minutes or until the potatoes are soft.
3. Use an immersion blender or transfer the soup to a blender to puree until smooth.
4. Return the pureed soup to the pot, add the heavy cream, and heat over low heat.
5. Season with salt and pepper to taste.
6. Serve hot, garnished with chopped fresh chives.

Minestrone Soup

Ingredients:

- 1 onion, chopped
- 2 garlic cloves, minced
- 2 carrots, peeled and chopped
- 2 celery stalks, chopped
- 1 zucchini, chopped
- 1 can diced tomatoes
- 4 cups vegetable broth
- 1 teaspoon dried oregano
- 1/2 cup small pasta (such as elbow macaroni or ditalini)
- Salt and pepper to taste
- Grated Parmesan cheese, for garnish

Instructions:

1. In a large pot, sauté the chopped onion and minced garlic in a tablespoon of olive oil until softened.
2. Add the chopped carrots, chopped celery, chopped zucchini, canned diced tomatoes, vegetable broth, and dried oregano to the pot, and bring to a boil. Reduce heat and let simmer for about 25 minutes.
3. Add the small pasta to the pot and let cook for an additional 10-15 minutes or until the pasta is tender.
4. Season with salt and pepper to taste.
5. Serve hot, garnished with grated Parmesan cheese.

Thai Coconut Curry Soup

Ingredients:

- 1 tablespoon vegetable oil
- 1 onion, chopped
- 2 garlic cloves, minced
- 1 red bell pepper, chopped
- 1 tablespoon Thai red curry paste
- 4 cups vegetable broth
- 1 can coconut milk
- 1 cup chopped kale
- Juice of 1 lime
- Salt and pepper to taste
- Chopped fresh cilantro, for garnish

Instructions:

1. Heat the vegetable oil in a large pot over medium heat. Add the chopped onion, minced garlic, and chopped red bell pepper and sauté until softened, about 5 minutes.
2. Add the Thai red curry paste to the pot and stir to combine. Cook for 1-2 minutes until fragrant.
3. Add the vegetable broth and coconut milk to the pot and bring to a simmer.
4. Add the chopped kale and let simmer for about 5 minutes until the kale is wilted.
5. Add the lime juice and season with salt and pepper to taste.
6. Serve hot, garnished with chopped fresh cilantro.

Butternut Squash Soup with Apple and Sage

Ingredients:

- 1 butternut squash, peeled, seeded, and chopped
- 2 apples, peeled, cored, and chopped
- 1 onion, chopped
- 4 cups vegetable broth
- 1 teaspoon dried sage
- 1/4 cup heavy cream
- Salt and pepper to taste
- Toasted pumpkin seeds, for garnish

Instructions:

1. In a large pot, sauté the chopped butternut squash, chopped apples, and chopped onion in a tablespoon of olive oil until softened.
2. Add the vegetable broth and dried sage to the pot, and bring to a boil. Reduce heat and let simmer for about 25 minutes or until the vegetables are soft.
3. Use an immersion blender or transfer the soup to a blender to puree until smooth.
4. Return the pureed soup to the pot, add the heavy cream, and heat over low heat.
5. Season with salt and pepper to taste.
6. Serve hot, garnished with toasted pumpkin seeds.

Creamy Mushroom and Wild Rice Soup

Ingredients:

- 1 onion, chopped
- 2 garlic cloves, minced
- 8 ounces sliced mushrooms
- 4 cups vegetable broth
- 1/2 cup wild rice
- 1/2 cup heavy cream
- Salt and pepper to taste
- Chopped fresh parsley, for garnish

Instructions:

1. In a large pot, sauté the chopped onion, minced garlic, and sliced mushrooms in a tablespoon of olive oil until softened.
2. Add the vegetable broth and wild rice to the pot, and bring to a boil. Reduce heat and let simmer for about 45 minutes or until the wild rice is tender.
3. Use an immersion blender or transfer about half of the soup to a blender to puree until smooth. Return the pureed soup to the pot.
4. Add the heavy cream and heat over low heat.
5. Season with salt and pepper to taste.
6. Serve hot, garnished with chopped fresh parsley.

Curried Cauliflower Soup

Ingredients:

- 1 head of cauliflower, chopped into florets
- 1 onion, chopped
- 2 garlic cloves, minced
- 1 tablespoon curry powder
- 4 cups vegetable broth
- 1 can coconut milk
- Salt and pepper to taste
- Chopped fresh cilantro, for garnish

Instructions:

1. In a large pot, sauté the chopped onion and minced garlic in a tablespoon of olive oil until softened.
2. Add the curry powder to the pot and stir to combine. Cook for 1-2 minutes until fragrant.
3. Add the chopped cauliflower and vegetable broth to the pot, and bring to a boil. Reduce heat and let simmer for about 20 minutes or until the cauliflower is tender.
4. Use an immersion blender or transfer the soup to a blender to puree until smooth.
5. Return the pureed soup to the pot and add the coconut milk. Heat over low heat.
6. Season with salt and pepper to taste.
7. Serve hot, garnished with chopped fresh cilantro.

Spinach and White Bean Soup

Ingredients:

- 1 onion, chopped
- 2 garlic cloves, minced
- 2 cans white beans, drained and rinsed
- 4 cups vegetable broth
- 1 cup chopped spinach
- 1 teaspoon dried oregano
- Salt and pepper to taste
- Grated Parmesan cheese, for garnish

Instructions:

1. In a large pot, sauté the chopped onion and minced garlic in a tablespoon of olive oil until softened.
2. Add the white beans, vegetable broth, chopped spinach, and dried oregano to the pot, and bring to a boil. Reduce heat and let simmer for about 10 minutes or until the spinach is wilted.
3. Use an immersion blender or transfer about half of the soup to a blender to puree until smooth. Return the pureed soup to the pot.
4. Season with salt and pepper to taste.
5. Serve hot, garnished with grated Parmesan cheese.

Corn and Potato Chowder

Ingredients:

- 2 tablespoons unsalted butter
- 1 onion, chopped
- 2 garlic cloves, minced
- 2 potatoes, peeled and chopped
- 4 cups vegetable broth
- 2 cups fresh or frozen corn kernels
- 1 cup milk
- Salt and pepper to taste
- Chopped fresh chives, for garnish

Instructions:

1. In a large pot, melt the unsalted butter over medium heat. Add the chopped onion and minced garlic and sauté until softened, about 5 minutes.
2. Add the chopped potatoes and vegetable broth to the pot, and bring to a boil. Reduce heat and let simmer for about 20 minutes or until the potatoes are tender.
3. Add the corn kernels and milk to the pot and cook for another 5-10 minutes.
4. Use an immersion blender or transfer about half of the soup to a blender to puree until smooth. Return the pureed soup to the pot.
5. Season with salt and pepper to taste.
6. Serve hot, garnished with chopped fresh chives.

Broccoli and Cheddar Soup

Ingredients:

- 1 tablespoon butter
- 1 onion, chopped
- 2 garlic cloves, minced
- 2 cups broccoli florets
- 4 cups vegetable broth
- 1/2 cup heavy cream
- 1 cup shredded cheddar cheese
- Salt and pepper to taste

Instructions:

1. In a large pot, melt the butter over medium heat. Add the chopped onion and minced garlic and sauté until softened, about 5 minutes.
2. Add the broccoli florets and vegetable broth to the pot and bring to a boil. Reduce heat and let simmer for about 20 minutes or until the broccoli is tender.
3. Use an immersion blender or transfer the soup to a blender to puree until smooth.
4. Return the pureed soup to the pot, add the heavy cream and shredded cheddar cheese, and heat over low heat until the cheese is melted and the soup is heated through.
5. Season with salt and pepper to taste.
6. Serve hot.

Mexican Tortilla Soup

Ingredients:

- 1 tablespoon vegetable oil
- 1 onion, chopped
- 2 garlic cloves, minced
- 1 red bell pepper, chopped
- 1 jalapeño pepper, seeded and chopped
- 4 cups vegetable broth
- 1 can diced tomatoes
- 1 cup frozen corn
- 1 teaspoon chili powder
- 1/2 teaspoon cumin
- Salt and pepper to taste
- Crushed tortilla chips, chopped fresh cilantro, and sliced avocado, for garnish

Instructions:

1. Heat the vegetable oil in a large pot over medium heat. Add the chopped onion, minced garlic, chopped red bell pepper, and chopped jalapeño pepper and sauté until softened, about 5 minutes.
2. Add the vegetable broth, diced tomatoes, frozen corn, chili powder, and cumin to the pot and bring to a boil. Reduce heat and let simmer for about 15 minutes.
3. Season with salt and pepper to taste.

4. Serve hot, garnished with crushed tortilla chips, chopped fresh cilantro, and sliced avocado.

Cauliflower and Chickpea Soup

Ingredients:

- 1 tablespoon olive oil
- 1 onion, chopped
- 2 garlic cloves, minced
- 1 head of cauliflower, chopped into small florets
- 1 can chickpeas, drained and rinsed
- 4 cups vegetable broth
- 1 teaspoon ground cumin
- 1/2 teaspoon paprika
- Salt and pepper to taste
- Chopped fresh parsley, for garnish

Instructions:

1. In a large pot, heat the olive oil over medium heat. Add the chopped onion and minced garlic and sauté until softened, about 5 minutes.
2. Add the chopped cauliflower, chickpeas, vegetable broth, ground cumin, and paprika to the pot and bring to a boil.

Reduce heat and let simmer for about 15 minutes or until the cauliflower is tender.

3. Use an immersion blender or transfer about half of the soup to a blender to puree until smooth. Return the pureed soup to the pot.
4. Heat the soup over low heat until heated through.
5. Season with salt and pepper to taste.
6. Serve hot, garnished with chopped fresh parsley.

Red Lentil and Spinach Soup

Ingredients:

- 1 tablespoon olive oil
- 1 onion, chopped
- 2 garlic cloves, minced
- 1 cup red lentils, rinsed
- 4 cups vegetable broth
- 2 cups chopped spinach
- 1 teaspoon ground cumin
- 1/2 teaspoon ground coriander
- Salt and pepper to taste
- Lemon wedges, for serving

Instructions:

1. In a large pot, heat the olive oil over medium heat. Add the chopped onion and minced garlic and sauté until softened, about 5 minutes.
2. Add the rinsed red lentils, vegetable broth, chopped spinach, ground cumin, and ground coriander to the pot and bring to a boil. Reduce heat and let simmer for about 20 minutes or until the lentils are tender.
3. Use an immersion blender or transfer about half of the soup to a blender to puree until smooth. Return the pureed soup to the pot.
4. Heat the soup over low heat until heated through.
5. Season with salt and pepper to taste.
6. Serve hot, with lemon wedges for squeezing over each serving.

Potato and Corn Chowder

Ingredients:

- 2 tablespoons butter
- 1 onion, chopped
- 2 garlic cloves, minced
- 2 potatoes, peeled and chopped
- 4 cups vegetable broth
- 1 can corn, drained
- 1 cup milk or non-dairy milk

- Salt and pepper to taste
- Chopped fresh chives, for garnish

Instructions:

1. In a large pot, melt the butter over medium heat. Add the chopped onion and minced garlic and sauté until softened, about 5 minutes.
2. Add the chopped potatoes, vegetable broth, and drained corn to the pot and bring to a boil. Reduce heat and let simmer for about 20 minutes or until the potatoes are tender.
3. Use an immersion blender or transfer about half of the soup to a blender to puree until smooth. Return the pureed soup to the pot.
4. Add the milk or non-dairy milk to the pot and heat over low heat until heated through.
5. Season with salt and pepper to taste.
6. Serve hot, garnished with chopped fresh chives.

Creamy Zucchini Soup

Ingredients:

- 4 medium zucchinis, chopped
- 1 large onion, chopped
- 2 garlic cloves, minced

- 4 cups vegetable broth
- 1/2 cup heavy cream
- 2 tablespoons olive oil
- Salt and pepper to taste

Instructions:

1. In a large pot, heat olive oil over medium heat.
2. Add onion and garlic and cook until onion is translucent.
3. Add zucchini and vegetable broth to the pot. Bring to a boil and reduce heat to low. Cover and simmer for 15-20 minutes or until the zucchini is soft.
4. Remove from heat and let cool for a few minutes.
5. Use an immersion blender or transfer to a blender to puree the soup until smooth.
6. Return to the pot and stir in heavy cream.
7. Season with salt and pepper to taste.

Sweet Potato and Kale Soup

Ingredients:

- 2 large sweet potatoes, peeled and chopped
- 1 large onion, chopped
- 2 garlic cloves, minced
- 4 cups vegetable broth

- 1 bunch kale, chopped
- 1/2 teaspoon ground cinnamon
- 1/4 teaspoon ground nutmeg
- 2 tablespoons olive oil
- Salt and pepper to taste

Instructions:

1. In a large pot, heat olive oil over medium heat.
2. Add onion and garlic and cook until onion is translucent.
3. Add sweet potatoes and vegetable broth to the pot. Bring to a boil and reduce heat to low. Cover and simmer for 20-25 minutes or until sweet potatoes are tender.
4. Add kale to the pot and cook until wilted, about 5-7 minutes.
5. Remove from heat and let cool for a few minutes.
6. Use an immersion blender or transfer to a blender to puree the soup until smooth.
7. Return to the pot and stir in cinnamon and nutmeg.
8. Season with salt and pepper to taste.

Chickpea and Vegetable Soup

Ingredients:

- 1 can chickpeas, drained and rinsed
- 2 carrots, chopped
- 2 celery stalks, chopped
- 1 large onion, chopped
- 2 garlic cloves, minced
- 4 cups vegetable broth
- 1 tablespoon tomato paste
- 1 teaspoon dried oregano
- 1 teaspoon dried basil
- 2 tablespoons olive oil
- Salt and pepper to taste

Instructions:

1. In a large pot, heat olive oil over medium heat.
2. Add onion and garlic and cook until onion is translucent.
3. Add carrots, celery, and chickpeas to the pot. Stir to combine.
4. Add vegetable broth, tomato paste, oregano, and basil to the pot. Bring to a boil and reduce heat to low. Cover and simmer for 20-25 minutes or until vegetables are tender.
5. Remove from heat and let cool for a few minutes.
6. Use an immersion blender or transfer to a blender to puree the soup until smooth.

7. Return to the pot and season with salt and pepper to taste.

Moroccan Spiced Carrot Soup

Ingredients:

- 1 tablespoon olive oil
- 1 onion, chopped
- 2 garlic cloves, minced
- 1 teaspoon ground cumin
- 1 teaspoon ground coriander
- 1/2 teaspoon ground cinnamon
- 4 cups carrots, chopped
- 4 cups vegetable broth
- Salt and pepper, to taste
- 1/4 cup chopped fresh cilantro

Directions:

1. In a large pot, heat the olive oil over medium heat.
2. Add the onion and garlic and sauté until soft and translucent, about 5 minutes.
3. Add the cumin, coriander, and cinnamon and stir to coat the onions and garlic.

4. Add the chopped carrots and vegetable broth to the pot and bring to a boil.
5. Reduce heat and simmer until the carrots are soft, about 20-25 minutes.
6. Use an immersion blender or transfer the soup to a blender and blend until smooth.
7. Season with salt and pepper to taste.
8. Serve hot with chopped cilantro on top.

Creamy Cauliflower Soup

Ingredients:

- 1 tablespoon olive oil
- 1 onion, chopped
- 3 garlic cloves, minced
- 1 head of cauliflower, chopped
- 4 cups vegetable broth
- Salt and pepper, to taste
- 1/2 cup heavy cream
- 1/4 cup chopped fresh parsley

Directions:

1. In a large pot, heat the olive oil over medium heat.

2. Add the onion and garlic and sauté until soft and translucent, about 5 minutes.
3. Add the chopped cauliflower and vegetable broth to the pot and bring to a boil.
4. Reduce heat and simmer until the cauliflower is soft, about 20-25 minutes.
5. Use an immersion blender or transfer the soup to a blender and blend until smooth.
6. Stir in the heavy cream and season with salt and pepper to taste.
7. Serve hot with chopped parsley on top.

Italian Wedding Soup

Ingredients:

- 1 tablespoon olive oil
- 1 onion, chopped
- 3 garlic cloves, minced
- 6 cups vegetable broth
- 1 cup small pasta (such as orzo or ditalini)
- 1 head of escarole, chopped
- 1 can of cannellini beans, drained and rinsed
- Salt and pepper, to taste
- 1/4 cup grated Parmesan cheese

Directions:

1. In a large pot, heat the olive oil over medium heat.
2. Add the onion and garlic and sauté until soft and translucent, about 5 minutes.
3. Add the vegetable broth to the pot and bring to a boil.
4. Add the pasta and cook according to package instructions.
5. Add the chopped escarole and cannellini beans to the pot and simmer until the escarole is wilted, about 5 minutes.
6. Season with salt and pepper to taste.
7. Serve hot with grated Parmesan cheese on top.

Vegetarian Borscht Soup

Ingredients:

- 4 medium beets, peeled and chopped
- 1 large onion, chopped
- 3 medium carrots, chopped
- 3 cups vegetable broth
- 2 cups water
- 1 tablespoon olive oil
- 2 tablespoons lemon juice
- Salt and pepper to taste
- 1/2 cup sour cream (optional)
- Fresh dill (for garnish)

Instructions:

1. Heat the olive oil in a large pot over medium heat.
2. Add the onions and sauté until softened, about 5 minutes.
3. Add the beets and carrots, and cook for another 5 minutes.
4. Pour in the vegetable broth and water, and bring to a boil.
5. Reduce the heat and let the soup simmer for 20-25 minutes or until the beets and carrots are tender.
6. Remove the pot from the heat and stir in the lemon juice, salt, and pepper.
7. Serve hot, topped with a dollop of sour cream and fresh dill.

Tomato and White Bean Soup

Ingredients:

- 2 cans white beans, drained and rinsed
- 2 cans diced tomatoes
- 1 onion, chopped
- 4 cloves garlic, minced
- 4 cups vegetable broth
- 1 tablespoon olive oil

- 1 tablespoon dried basil
- Salt and pepper to taste

Instructions:

1. Heat the olive oil in a large pot over medium heat.
2. Add the onions and sauté until softened, about 5 minutes.
3. Add the garlic and cook for another 1-2 minutes.
4. Pour in the vegetable broth and canned tomatoes, and bring to a boil.
5. Add the white beans and dried basil, and reduce the heat to let the soup simmer for 20-25 minutes.
6. Use an immersion blender or transfer the soup to a blender and blend until smooth.
7. Season with salt and pepper to taste.
8. Serve hot with a crusty bread.

Vegan Broccoli Soup

Ingredients:

- 1 head of broccoli, chopped into florets
- 1 onion, chopped
- 2 cloves garlic, minced
- 4 cups vegetable broth

- 1 tablespoon olive oil
- 1/2 cup nutritional yeast
- Salt and pepper to taste

Instructions:

1. Heat the olive oil in a large pot over medium heat.
2. Add the onions and sauté until softened, about 5 minutes.
3. Add the garlic and cook for another 1-2 minutes.
4. Pour in the vegetable broth and add the broccoli florets.
5. Bring to a boil, then reduce the heat and let the soup simmer for 20-25 minutes or until the broccoli is tender.
6. Use an immersion blender or transfer the soup to a blender and blend until smooth.
7. Stir in the nutritional yeast, salt, and pepper.
8. Serve hot with some crusty bread or croutons.

Pasta and Grains

Spaghetti with Roasted Vegetables and Feta

Ingredients:

- 8 oz. spaghetti
- 1 zucchini, chopped
- 1 red bell pepper, chopped
- 1/2 red onion, chopped
- 2 tbsp. olive oil
- 4 oz. feta cheese, crumbled
- 2 tbsp. chopped fresh parsley
- 1 lemon, juiced
- Salt and pepper to taste

Instructions:

1. Cook spaghetti according to package directions.
2. Toss chopped zucchini, red bell pepper, and red onion with olive oil and roast in the oven until tender.
3. Mix the roasted veggies with cooked spaghetti, crumbled feta cheese, chopped fresh parsley, and a squeeze of lemon juice.
4. Season with salt and pepper to taste.

Quinoa and Black Bean Salad

Ingredients:

- 1 cup quinoa
- 1 red onion, diced
- 2 cloves garlic, minced
- 1 can black beans, drained and rinsed
- 1 large tomato, diced
- 1/4 cup chopped fresh cilantro
- 2 tbsp. lime juice
- Salt and pepper to taste

Instructions:

1. Cook quinoa according to package directions.
2. In a separate pan, sauté diced red onion and minced garlic until soft.
3. Add cooked black beans, cooked quinoa, diced tomatoes, chopped fresh cilantro, and lime juice to the pan.
4. Toss everything together and season with salt and pepper to taste.
5. Serve the salad cold or at room temperature.

Brown Rice and Vegetable Stir-Fry

Ingredients:

- 2 cups cooked brown rice
- 1 red bell pepper, sliced
- 1 zucchini, sliced
- 1 yellow squash, sliced
- 1 cup broccoli florets
- 2 cloves garlic, minced
- 2 tbsp. olive oil
- 1/4 cup soy sauce
- 2 tbsp. honey
- Salt and pepper to taste

Instructions:

1. In a large pan or wok, heat olive oil over medium-high heat.
2. Add sliced red bell pepper, zucchini, yellow squash, and broccoli florets. Sauté until tender.
3. Add minced garlic and sauté for another minute.
4. Add cooked brown rice to the pan and stir to combine with the vegetables.
5. In a small bowl, whisk together soy sauce and honey. Pour over the rice and vegetable mixture and stir to coat.
6. Season with salt and pepper to taste.

Chickpea and Orzo Salad

Ingredients:

- 1 cup orzo pasta
- 1 can chickpeas, drained and rinsed
- 1/2 red onion, diced
- 1/2 cucumber, diced
- 1/2 cup cherry tomatoes, halved
- 1/4 cup feta cheese, crumbled
- 2 tablespoons chopped fresh parsley
- 1/4 cup olive oil
- 2 tablespoons red wine vinegar
- Salt and pepper to taste

Instructions:

1. Cook the orzo according to package instructions until al dente. Drain and rinse with cold water.
2. In a large bowl, combine the orzo, chickpeas, red onion, cucumber, cherry tomatoes, feta cheese, and parsley.
3. In a small bowl, whisk together the olive oil, red wine vinegar, salt, and pepper. Pour the dressing over the salad and toss to combine.
4. Chill the salad for at least 30 minutes before serving.

Spiced Lentil and Couscous Salad

Ingredients:

- 1 cup couscous
- 2 cups vegetable broth
- 1 can lentils, drained and rinsed
- 1/2 red onion, diced
- 1/2 red bell pepper, diced
- 1/2 yellow bell pepper, diced
- 1/2 teaspoon cumin
- 1/2 teaspoon smoked paprika
- 1/4 teaspoon cinnamon
- 2 tablespoons chopped fresh parsley
- 1/4 cup olive oil
- 2 tablespoons lemon juice
- Salt and pepper to taste

Instructions:

1. In a medium saucepan, bring the vegetable broth to a boil. Add the couscous, cover the pan, and remove from heat. Let the couscous steam for 10 minutes.
2. In a large bowl, combine the cooked couscous, lentils, red onion, red and yellow bell peppers, cumin, smoked paprika, cinnamon, and parsley.
3. In a small bowl, whisk together the olive oil, lemon juice, salt, and pepper. Pour the dressing over the salad and toss to combine.
4. Chill the salad for at least 30 minutes before serving.

Mushroom and Barley Soup

Ingredients:

- 1 cup pearl barley
- 6 cups vegetable broth
- 2 tablespoons olive oil
- 1 onion, diced
- 2 garlic cloves, minced
- 8 ounces mushrooms, sliced
- 1 carrot, diced
- 1 celery stalk, diced
- 1 teaspoon dried thyme
- Salt and pepper to taste

Instructions:

1. In a large pot, heat the olive oil over medium heat. Add the onion and garlic and sauté for 2-3 minutes.
2. Add the mushrooms, carrot, and celery to the pot and cook until the vegetables are slightly softened, about 5-7 minutes.
3. Add the pearl barley, vegetable broth, thyme, salt, and pepper to the pot. Bring to a boil, then reduce the heat and simmer for 45 minutes or until the barley is tender.
4. Serve the soup hot, garnished with fresh parsley if desired.

Mediterranean Farro Salad

Ingredients:

- 1 cup farro
- 2 cups water
- 1/2 cup chopped cucumber
- 1/2 cup cherry tomatoes, halved
- 1/2 cup chopped Kalamata olives
- 1/4 cup chopped red onion
- 1/4 cup crumbled feta cheese
- 1/4 cup chopped fresh parsley
- 2 tablespoons olive oil
- 2 tablespoons lemon juice
- 1 teaspoon honey
- Salt and pepper, to taste

Instructions:

1. Rinse the farro and add it to a pot with 2 cups of water. Bring to a boil, then reduce heat and simmer for 20-25 minutes, or until the farro is tender but still chewy.
2. Drain any excess water from the farro and transfer it to a large mixing bowl.
3. Add the cucumber, cherry tomatoes, Kalamata olives, red onion, feta cheese, and parsley to the bowl with the farro.
4. In a small bowl, whisk together the olive oil, lemon juice, honey, salt, and pepper until well combined.
5. Pour the dressing over the salad and toss to combine.

6. Serve immediately or chill in the refrigerator until ready to serve.

Cheesy Baked Ziti

Ingredients:

- 1 pound ziti pasta
- 1 jar (24 ounces) marinara sauce
- 1 cup ricotta cheese
- 1/2 cup grated Parmesan cheese
- 2 cups shredded mozzarella cheese
- Salt and pepper, to taste

Instructions:

1. Preheat the oven to 375°F (190°C).
2. Cook the ziti pasta according to package instructions until al dente.
3. Drain the pasta and transfer it to a large mixing bowl.
4. Add the marinara sauce, ricotta cheese, Parmesan cheese, and half of the shredded mozzarella cheese to the bowl with the pasta. Season with salt and pepper to taste and mix well.
5. Transfer the pasta mixture to a 9x13 inch baking dish and top with the remaining shredded mozzarella cheese.
6. Bake for 20-25 minutes, or until the cheese is melted and bubbly.

7. Serve hot.

Roasted Butternut Squash and Barley Risotto

Ingredients:

- 1 butternut squash, peeled and diced into small cubes
- 1 tablespoon olive oil
- Salt and pepper, to taste
- 1 cup pearl barley
- 3 cups vegetable broth
- 1/2 cup grated Parmesan cheese
- 2 tablespoons butter
- 2 tablespoons chopped fresh sage leaves

Instructions:

1. Preheat the oven to 400°F (200°C).
2. Toss the diced butternut squash with olive oil, salt, and pepper and spread it out in a single layer on a baking sheet.
3. Roast the squash in the oven for 20-25 minutes, or until tender and lightly browned.
4. In a large pot, bring the vegetable broth to a simmer over medium heat.

5. Add the pearl barley to the pot and stir well. Cover and let simmer for 20-25 minutes, or until the barley is tender.
6. Add the roasted butternut squash to the pot with the barley and stir well.
7. Stir in the grated Parmesan cheese, butter, and chopped sage leaves until well combined.
8. Serve hot.

Caprese Farro Salad

Ingredients:

- 1 cup farro, uncooked
- 2 cups cherry tomatoes, halved
- 1 cup fresh mozzarella, cubed
- 1/4 cup fresh basil, chopped
- 2 tablespoons balsamic vinegar
- 2 tablespoons olive oil
- Salt and pepper, to taste

Instructions:

1. Cook farro according to package instructions and let it cool.

2. In a large bowl, mix the cooled farro with cherry tomatoes, mozzarella, and fresh basil.
3. In a separate bowl, whisk together balsamic vinegar and olive oil. Drizzle over the salad and toss to combine.
4. Season with salt and pepper to taste. Serve chilled.

Creamy Avocado and Spelt Salad

Ingredients:

- 2 cups spelt, cooked
- 1 avocado, diced
- 1/4 cup red onion, diced
- 1/4 cup fresh parsley, chopped
- 1/4 cup fresh lemon juice
- 1/4 cup olive oil
- Salt and pepper, to taste

Instructions:

1. Cook spelt according to package instructions and let it cool.
2. In a large bowl, mix the cooled spelt with diced avocado, red onion, and fresh parsley.
3. In a separate bowl, whisk together lemon juice and olive oil. Add to the salad and toss to combine.
4. Season with salt and pepper to taste. Serve chilled.

Pesto Gnocchi with Roasted Vegetables

Ingredients:

- 1 pound gnocchi, uncooked
- 2 cups mixed vegetables (zucchini, bell peppers, onions), chopped
- 1/4 cup pesto
- 1/4 cup Parmesan cheese, grated
- 2 tablespoons olive oil
- Salt and pepper, to taste

Instructions:

1. Preheat oven to 400°F (200°C). Place chopped vegetables on a baking sheet and drizzle with olive oil. Roast for 20-25 minutes, until tender.
2. Cook gnocchi according to package instructions and drain.
3. In a large bowl, mix the cooked gnocchi with roasted vegetables, pesto, and grated Parmesan cheese.
4. Season with salt and pepper to taste. Serve warm.

Lemon Parmesan Pasta with Asparagus and Peas

Ingredients:

- 8 oz. pasta
- 1 bunch asparagus, trimmed and cut into 1-inch pieces
- 1 cup frozen peas
- 1/4 cup grated Parmesan cheese
- 2 tbsp. butter
- 1 lemon, zested and juiced
- Salt and pepper, to taste

Instructions:

1. Cook pasta according to package directions until al dente. Drain and set aside.
2. In a separate pot, blanch asparagus and peas in boiling water for 2-3 minutes, then drain and set aside.
3. In a large skillet, melt butter over medium heat. Add the cooked pasta, asparagus, peas, lemon zest, and lemon juice. Toss to combine.
4. Sprinkle Parmesan cheese over the pasta and vegetables, and toss again until the cheese is melted and the vegetables are coated.
5. Season with salt and pepper to taste. Serve hot.

Spicy Peanut Noodles with Tofu

Ingredients:

- 8 oz. spaghetti
- 1/2 cup peanut butter
- 2 tbsp. soy sauce
- 2 tbsp. rice vinegar
- 2 tbsp. sesame oil
- 1 tbsp. honey
- 1/2 tsp. red pepper flakes
- 1 block extra-firm tofu, pressed and cubed
- 2 green onions, thinly sliced
- 1/4 cup chopped cilantro
- Lime wedges, for serving

Instructions:

1. Cook spaghetti according to package directions until al dente. Drain and set aside.
2. In a bowl, whisk together peanut butter, soy sauce, rice vinegar, sesame oil, honey, and red pepper flakes.
3. In a separate skillet, sauté cubed tofu until lightly browned.
4. Add the peanut sauce to the skillet with the tofu, and cook for 1-2 minutes until heated through.
5. Toss cooked spaghetti with the peanut sauce and tofu mixture. Top with sliced green onions and chopped cilantro.
6. Serve with lime wedges for squeezing over the noodles.

Butternut Squash and Kale Farro Risotto

Ingredients:

- 1 cup farro
- 1 small butternut squash, peeled, seeded, and cut into small cubes
- 2 cups kale, chopped
- 1 onion, chopped
- 2 cloves garlic, minced
- 1/2 cup grated Parmesan cheese
- 2 tbsp. olive oil
- Salt and pepper, to taste

Instructions:

1. Preheat the oven to 375°F (190°C).
2. In a large pot, cook farro according to package directions until tender. Drain and set aside.
3. Toss butternut squash with 1 tbsp. of olive oil and spread out onto a baking sheet. Roast in the oven for 25-30 minutes, or until tender and golden brown.
4. In a separate pan, heat remaining olive oil over medium heat. Add onion and garlic, and sauté until onion is translucent.
5. Add cooked farro to the pan with the onion and garlic. Stir in roasted butternut squash and chopped kale.
6. Cook for 3-5 minutes until kale is wilted and farro is heated through.

7. Add Parmesan cheese to the pan, and stir until melted and well combined.
8. Season with salt and pepper to taste. Serve hot.

One-Pot Tomato Basil Pasta

Ingredients:

- 1 pound spaghetti
- 4 cups vegetable broth
- 1 can (28 oz) crushed tomatoes
- 1 onion, chopped
- 4 cloves garlic, minced
- 1/4 cup fresh basil, chopped
- 1 teaspoon red pepper flakes
- Salt and pepper to taste
- Parmesan cheese, grated

Instructions:

1. In a large pot, add spaghetti, vegetable broth, crushed tomatoes, onion, garlic, basil, and red pepper flakes.
2. Bring the mixture to a boil, then reduce the heat to medium-low and cook for about 10-12 minutes or until the pasta is cooked to your liking.
3. Season with salt and pepper to taste.

4. Serve with grated Parmesan cheese on top.

Vegan Chickpea Alfredo

Ingredients:

- 1 pound fettuccine
- 1 can (15 oz) chickpeas, drained and rinsed
- 1 cup vegetable broth
- 1/2 cup nutritional yeast
- 2 cloves garlic, minced
- 2 tablespoons olive oil
- Salt and pepper to taste
- Fresh parsley, chopped

Instructions:

1. Cook fettuccine according to package instructions.
2. In a blender, combine chickpeas, vegetable broth, nutritional yeast, garlic, and olive oil. Blend until smooth.
3. In a large saucepan, add the blended mixture and heat over medium heat.
4. Add salt and pepper to taste.
5. Once the sauce is heated through, add the cooked fettuccine and stir until the pasta is coated in the sauce.
6. Serve with fresh parsley on top.

Mexican Quinoa Stew

Ingredients:

- 1 cup quinoa
- 1 can (15 oz) black beans, drained and rinsed
- 1 can (14.5 oz) diced tomatoes
- 1 onion, chopped
- 1 bell pepper, chopped
- 2 cloves garlic, minced
- 2 cups vegetable broth
- 2 teaspoons cumin
- 2 teaspoons chili powder
- Salt and pepper to taste
- Avocado, chopped
- Fresh cilantro, chopped

Instructions:

1. In a large pot, add quinoa, black beans, diced tomatoes, onion, bell pepper, garlic, vegetable broth, cumin, and chili powder.
2. Bring the mixture to a boil, then reduce the heat to medium-low and cook for about 20-25 minutes or until the quinoa is cooked and the vegetables are tender.
3. Season with salt and pepper to taste.
4. Serve with chopped avocado and fresh cilantro on top.

Spinach and Ricotta Stuffed Shells

Ingredients:

- 1 box of jumbo pasta shells
- 2 cups of ricotta cheese
- 2 cups of chopped spinach
- 1 egg
- 1/2 cup of grated parmesan cheese
- 2 cloves of garlic, minced
- Salt and pepper to taste
- 2 cups of marinara sauce
- Fresh basil leaves for garnish

Instructions:

1. Preheat the oven to 375°F.
2. Cook the pasta shells according to package instructions until they are al dente.
3. In a bowl, mix together the ricotta cheese, spinach, egg, parmesan cheese, garlic, salt, and pepper.
4. Stuff the mixture into each pasta shell and place them in a 9x13 inch baking dish.
5. Pour the marinara sauce over the stuffed shells and cover the dish with foil.
6. Bake for 25-30 minutes, then remove the foil and bake for an additional 5-10 minutes until the cheese is melted and bubbly.
7. Garnish with fresh basil leaves and serve hot.

Mushroom and Spinach Linguine

Ingredients:

- 1 lb. linguine pasta
- 2 tablespoons of olive oil
- 1 lb. of sliced mushrooms
- 2 cloves of garlic, minced
- 2 cups of chopped spinach
- 1/2 cup of vegetable broth
- 1/4 cup of grated parmesan cheese
- Salt and pepper to taste
- Fresh parsley leaves for garnish

Instructions:

1. Cook the pasta according to package instructions until it is al dente, then drain and set aside.
2. Heat the olive oil in a large skillet over medium-high heat.
3. Add the mushrooms and garlic and cook until the mushrooms are tender and the liquid has evaporated.
4. Add the chopped spinach and vegetable broth to the skillet and cook for an additional 2-3 minutes until the spinach is wilted.
5. Season with salt and pepper to taste.
6. Add the cooked pasta to the skillet and toss to combine with the mushroom and spinach mixture.
7. Top with grated parmesan cheese and fresh parsley leaves, and serve hot.

Greek Salad with Orzo

Ingredients:

- 1 cup of orzo pasta
- 2 tablespoons of olive oil
- 1/2 red onion, thinly sliced
- 1 red bell pepper, diced
- 1 cucumber, diced
- 1 cup of cherry tomatoes, halved
- 1/2 cup of crumbled feta cheese
- 1/4 cup of chopped kalamata olives
- 1/4 cup of chopped fresh parsley
- 2 tablespoons of lemon juice
- Salt and pepper to taste

Instructions:

1. Cook the orzo according to package instructions until it is al dente, then drain and rinse with cold water.
2. Heat the olive oil in a large skillet over medium-high heat.
3. Add the red onion and red bell pepper to the skillet and sauté for 5-7 minutes until they are tender.
4. In a large bowl, combine the cooked orzo, sautéed vegetables, cucumber, cherry tomatoes, feta cheese, kalamata olives, and chopped parsley.
5. Drizzle with lemon juice and season with salt and pepper to taste.
6. Toss the salad to combine all ingredients.

7. Serve chilled or at room temperature.

Lentil and Spinach Spaghetti

Ingredients:

- 8 oz. spaghetti
- 1 cup cooked lentils
- 2 cups fresh spinach leaves
- 1/4 cup chopped red onion
- 2 cloves garlic, minced
- 2 tbsp. olive oil
- Salt and pepper, to taste
- Grated Parmesan cheese (optional)

Instructions:

1. Cook spaghetti according to package instructions.
2. Heat olive oil in a skillet over medium heat.
3. Add minced garlic and red onion and cook until fragrant.
4. Add cooked lentils and spinach to the skillet and cook until spinach wilts.
5. Add salt and pepper to taste.
6. Serve lentil and spinach mixture over spaghetti and top with grated Parmesan cheese (optional).

Wild Rice and Mushroom Pilaf

Ingredients:

- 1 cup wild rice
- 2 cups vegetable broth
- 1 tbsp. olive oil
- 1 onion, chopped
- 2 cloves garlic, minced
- 8 oz. mushrooms, sliced
- Salt and pepper, to taste
- Chopped fresh parsley (optional)

Instructions:

1. Rinse wild rice and cook in vegetable broth according to package instructions.
2. Heat olive oil in a skillet over medium heat.
3. Add chopped onion and minced garlic and cook until fragrant.
4. Add sliced mushrooms to the skillet and cook until they release their moisture and turn brown.
5. Add cooked wild rice to the skillet and mix well.
6. Add salt and pepper to taste.
7. Serve wild rice and mushroom pilaf topped with chopped fresh parsley (optional).
8.

Chickpea and Vegetable Curry with Basmati Rice

Ingredients:

- 1 cup basmati rice
- 2 cups vegetable broth
- 1 tbsp. olive oil
- 1 onion, chopped
- 2 cloves garlic, minced
- 1 bell pepper, chopped
- 1 zucchini, chopped
- 1 can chickpeas, drained and rinsed
- 1 tbsp. curry powder
- Salt and pepper, to taste

Instructions:

1. Rinse basmati rice and cook in vegetable broth according to package instructions.
2. Heat olive oil in a skillet over medium heat.
3. Add chopped onion and minced garlic and cook until fragrant.
4. Add chopped bell pepper and zucchini to the skillet and cook until tender.
5. Add drained and rinsed chickpeas, curry powder, and salt and pepper to the skillet and mix well.
6. Serve chickpea and vegetable curry over basmati rice.

Desserts

Chocolate Avocado Mousse

Ingredients:

- 2 ripe avocados
- 1/2 cup cocoa powder
- 1/2 cup maple syrup
- 1 tsp vanilla extract
- Pinch of salt
- Fresh berries for topping

Instructions:

1. Cut the avocados in half and remove the pits.
2. Scoop the flesh of the avocados into a food processor.
3. Add the cocoa powder, maple syrup, vanilla extract, and salt to the food processor.
4. Blend the ingredients until smooth and creamy.
5. Divide the mousse into small bowls or ramekins.
6. Chill in the fridge for at least 1 hour.
7. Top with fresh berries before serving.

Vegan Banana Bread

Ingredients:

- 3 ripe bananas
- 1/3 cup melted coconut oil
- 1/2 cup brown sugar
- 1 tsp vanilla extract
- 1 1/2 cups all-purpose flour
- 1 tsp baking soda
- 1/4 tsp salt
- Cinnamon and nutmeg to taste

Instructions:

1. Preheat your oven to 350°F (180°C).
2. Mash the bananas in a large mixing bowl.
3. Add the melted coconut oil, brown sugar, and vanilla extract to the mixing bowl.
4. Mix until well combined.
5. In a separate mixing bowl, sift together the flour, baking soda, salt, cinnamon, and nutmeg.
6. Add the dry ingredients to the banana mixture and stir until just combined.
7. Pour the batter into a greased loaf pan.
8. Bake for 45-50 minutes, or until a toothpick inserted into the center of the bread comes out clean.
9. Let the bread cool before slicing and serving.

Vegan Chocolate Chip Cookies

Ingredients:

- 1/2 cup melted coconut oil
- 1/2 cup brown sugar
- 1/4 cup white sugar
- 1/4 cup unsweetened applesauce
- 1 tsp vanilla extract
- 1 3/4 cups all-purpose flour
- 1/2 tsp baking soda
- 1/2 tsp salt
- 1 cup vegan chocolate chips

Instructions:

1. Preheat your oven to 350°F (180°C).
2. In a mixing bowl, combine the melted coconut oil, brown sugar, and white sugar.
3. Add the unsweetened applesauce and vanilla extract to the mixing bowl and mix until well combined.
4. In a separate mixing bowl, sift together the flour, baking soda, and salt.
5. Add the dry ingredients to the wet mixture and stir until just combined.
6. Fold in the vegan chocolate chips.
7. Drop spoonful's of the dough onto a baking sheet lined with parchment paper.
8. Bake for 12-15 minutes, or until the edges are golden brown.

9. Let the cookies cool on the baking sheet for a few minutes before transferring them to a wire rack to cool completely.

Berry and Yogurt Parfait

Ingredients:

- 1 cup Greek yogurt
- 1 cup mixed berries (blueberries, strawberries, raspberries)
- 1/2 cup granola
- 2 tablespoons honey
- 1 teaspoon vanilla extract

Instructions:

1. In a small bowl, mix together the yogurt, honey, and vanilla extract.
2. In a separate bowl, mix together the berries.
3. In a glass or jar, layer the yogurt mixture, granola, and berries.
4. Repeat the layers until you fill the glass or jar.
5. Top with extra berries and granola as desired.
6. Serve chilled.

Fruit Salad with Mint Lime Dressing

Ingredients:

- 2 cups mixed fruit (cantaloupe, honeydew, pineapple, grapes, etc.)
- 1 tablespoon fresh lime juice
- 1 tablespoon honey
- 1 tablespoon chopped mint leaves

Instructions:

1. Cut the fruit into bite-sized pieces and add them to a large bowl.
2. In a separate small bowl, whisk together the lime juice, honey, and mint leaves to make the dressing.
3. Pour the dressing over the fruit and toss gently to combine.
4. Cover and chill for at least 30 minutes before serving.

Apple Cinnamon Oatmeal Cookies

Ingredients:

- 2 cups old-fashioned oats
- 1/2 cup all-purpose flour
- 1/2 teaspoon baking soda

- 1/2 teaspoon ground cinnamon
- 1/4 teaspoon salt
- 1/2 cup unsweetened applesauce
- 1/2 cup packed brown sugar
- 1/4 cup vegetable oil
- 1 egg
- 1 teaspoon vanilla extract

Instructions:

1. Preheat the oven to 350°F (180°C) and line a baking sheet with parchment paper.
2. In a medium bowl, whisk together the oats, flour, baking soda, cinnamon, and salt.
3. In a separate large bowl, whisk together the applesauce, brown sugar, vegetable oil, egg, and vanilla extract until smooth.
4. Add the dry ingredients to the wet ingredients and stir until just combined.
5. Drop the cookie dough by tablespoonfuls onto the prepared baking sheet, spacing them about 2 inches apart.
6. Bake for 12 to 15 minutes or until the edges are lightly golden brown.
7. Allow the cookies to cool on the baking sheet for 5 minutes before transferring them to a wire rack to cool completely.

Vegan Peanut Butter Chocolate Cake

Ingredients:

- 1 cup all-purpose flour
- 1/2 cup unsweetened cocoa powder
- 1 tsp baking powder
- 1/2 tsp baking soda
- 1/2 tsp salt
- 1/2 cup creamy peanut butter
- 1/2 cup maple syrup
- 1/2 cup unsweetened applesauce
- 1/2 cup unsweetened almond milk
- 1 tsp vanilla extract

Instructions:

1. Preheat the oven to 350°F (175°C).
2. Grease an 8-inch round cake pan.
3. In a medium bowl, whisk together the flour, cocoa powder, baking powder, baking soda, and salt.
4. In a large bowl, beat the peanut butter, maple syrup, and applesauce until smooth.
5. Add the almond milk and vanilla extract, and beat until well combined.
6. Gradually add the dry ingredients to the wet ingredients, and beat until well combined.
7. Pour the batter into the prepared pan.
8. Bake for 25-30 minutes, or until a toothpick inserted in the center of the cake comes out clean.

9. Let the cake cool in the pan for 5 minutes before transferring it to a wire rack to cool completely.

Vegan Strawberry Cheesecake

Ingredients:

For the crust:

- 1 1/2 cups graham cracker crumbs
- 1/4 cup coconut oil, melted
- 2 tbsp maple syrup

For the filling:

- 2 cups raw cashews, soaked overnight
- 1/2 cup coconut cream
- 1/2 cup maple syrup
- 1/4 cup coconut oil, melted
- 1/4 cup lemon juice
- 1 tsp vanilla extract
- 1 cup strawberries

Instructions:

1. Preheat the oven to 350°F (175°C).

2. In a bowl, mix together the graham cracker crumbs, coconut oil, and maple syrup until well combined.
3. Press the mixture into the bottom of a 9-inch springform pan.
4. Bake for 10 minutes, then let it cool completely.
5. In a blender, combine the soaked cashews, coconut cream, maple syrup, coconut oil, lemon juice, and vanilla extract. Blend until smooth.
6. Pour the mixture over the cooled crust and smooth the top.
7. Refrigerate for at least 4 hours or overnight.
8. Before serving, top with fresh sliced strawberries.

Vegan Blueberry Crisp

Ingredients:

- 4 cups fresh blueberries
- 1/4 cup maple syrup
- 1/2 cup all-purpose flour
- 1/2 cup rolled oats
- 1/2 cup chopped walnuts
- 1/4 cup coconut oil, melted
- 1/4 cup brown sugar
- 1 tsp ground cinnamon
- 1/4 tsp salt

Instructions:

1. Preheat the oven to 375°F (190°C).
2. In a 9x9 inch baking dish, mix together the blueberries and maple syrup until well combined.
3. In a medium bowl, mix together the flour, oats, walnuts, coconut oil, brown sugar, cinnamon, and salt until well combined.
4. Sprinkle the mixture over the blueberries.
5. Bake for 35-40 minutes, or until the topping is golden brown and the blueberries are bubbling.
6. Let cool for 10 minutes before serving. Serve warm with a scoop of vegan vanilla ice cream, if desired.

Lemon Blueberry Bars

Ingredients:

- 1 cup all-purpose flour
- 1/2 cup rolled oats
- 1/2 cup brown sugar
- 1/2 cup butter, softened
- 1/2 tsp baking powder
- 1/4 tsp salt
- 1 cup fresh blueberries
- 1/4 cup lemon juice

- 2 tbsp cornstarch
- 1/4 cup white sugar

Instructions:

1. Preheat oven to 375°F (190°C). Grease an 8-inch square baking dish.
2. In a bowl, combine flour, oats, brown sugar, butter, baking powder, and salt until crumbly.
3. Press 2 cups of the mixture into the bottom of the prepared baking dish.
4. In another bowl, mix together blueberries, lemon juice, cornstarch, and white sugar. Spread the blueberry mixture over the crust.
5. Sprinkle the remaining crumb mixture over the blueberry layer.
6. Bake for 35 to 40 minutes or until the top is light brown. Cool before cutting into squares.

Mango Coconut Rice Pudding

Ingredients:

- 1 cup uncooked white rice
- 2 cups water
- 1 can (14 oz) coconut milk

- 1/2 cup sugar
- 1/4 tsp salt
- 1 mango, peeled and chopped
- 1/4 cup shredded coconut

Instructions:

1. Rinse the rice and place it in a medium-sized saucepan with the water.
2. Bring to a boil over high heat, then reduce heat to low and simmer for 18-20 minutes, until the water is absorbed and the rice is cooked.
3. Stir in the coconut milk, sugar, and salt. Bring to a boil and then reduce heat to low. Simmer for 10 minutes, stirring occasionally.
4. Remove from heat and let it cool for 10 minutes. Stir in the chopped mango and shredded coconut.
5. Serve warm or cold.

Caramelized Pear and Walnut Tart

Ingredients:

- 1 sheet puff pastry, thawed
- 2 tbsp unsalted butter
- 2 tbsp brown sugar
- 1 tbsp honey
- 2 pears, cored and sliced

- 1/4 cup chopped walnuts

Instructions:

1. Preheat oven to 400°F (200°C). Line a baking sheet with parchment paper.
2. Roll out the puff pastry sheet and place it on the prepared baking sheet.
3. In a small saucepan, melt butter, brown sugar, and honey over low heat.
4. Arrange the sliced pears on top of the puff pastry, leaving a 1-inch border around the edges.
5. Drizzle the melted butter mixture over the pears and sprinkle with chopped walnuts.
6. Bake for 25-30 minutes, until the puff pastry is golden brown and the pears are caramelized.
7. Let cool for a few minutes before slicing and serving.

Vegan Chocolate Pudding

Ingredients:

- 1/2 cup cocoa powder
- 1/2 cup sugar
- 1/4 cup cornstarch
- 1/4 tsp salt

- 2 3/4 cups almond milk
- 1 tsp vanilla extract

Instructions:

1. In a medium saucepan, whisk together cocoa powder, sugar, cornstarch, and salt.
2. Slowly add almond milk, whisking constantly, until the mixture is smooth and no lumps remain.
3. Heat the mixture over medium heat, stirring constantly, until it thickens and begins to boil.
4. Continue cooking and stirring for 1-2 minutes more, then remove from heat.
5. Stir in vanilla extract.
6. Pour the pudding into individual serving dishes and chill in the refrigerator until set, about 2-3 hours.

Vegan Carrot Cake

Ingredients:

- 2 cups flour
- 2 tsp baking powder
- 1 tsp baking soda
- 1 tsp cinnamon
- 1/2 tsp nutmeg

- 1/4 tsp salt
- 1 1/2 cups grated carrots
- 1 cup brown sugar
- 1/2 cup vegetable oil
- 1/2 cup unsweetened applesauce
- 1 tsp vanilla extract
- 1 cup chopped walnuts (optional)

Instructions:

1. Preheat oven to 350°F (180°C) and grease a 9-inch (23cm) square baking dish.
2. In a large bowl, whisk together flour, baking powder, baking soda, cinnamon, nutmeg, and salt.
3. Add grated carrots, brown sugar, vegetable oil, applesauce, and vanilla extract, and stir until well combined.
4. Fold in chopped walnuts, if using.
5. Pour the batter into the prepared baking dish and bake for 35-40 minutes, or until a toothpick inserted in the center comes out clean.
6. Allow the cake to cool completely before slicing and serving.

Vegan Coconut Macaroons

Ingredients:

- 2 cups unsweetened shredded coconut
- 1/2 cup sugar
- 1/4 cup flour
- 1/4 tsp salt
- 1/2 cup aquafaba (liquid from canned chickpeas)
- 1 tsp vanilla extract

Instructions:

1. Preheat oven to 350°F (180°C) and line a baking sheet with parchment paper.
2. In a large bowl, whisk together shredded coconut, sugar, flour, and salt.
3. In a separate bowl, beat aquafaba and vanilla extract with an electric mixer until stiff peaks form, about 5-7 minutes.
4. Gently fold the aquafaba mixture into the coconut mixture until well combined.
5. Use a small cookie scoop or tablespoon to form the mixture into small balls, and place them on the prepared baking sheet.
6. Bake for 20-25 minutes, or until the macaroons are golden brown on the outside and slightly soft on the inside.

7. Allow the macaroons to cool on the baking sheet for 5 minutes before transferring them to a wire rack to cool completely.

Vegan Peach Cobbler

Ingredients:

- 4-5 ripe peaches, sliced
- 1/2 cup flour
- 1/2 cup rolled oats
- 1/4 cup brown sugar
- 1/4 cup coconut oil
- 1/4 tsp cinnamon
- 1/4 tsp nutmeg
- 1/4 tsp salt

Instructions:

1. Preheat the oven to 375°F.
2. Arrange the sliced peaches in a baking dish.
3. In a separate bowl, combine the flour, rolled oats, brown sugar, cinnamon, nutmeg, and salt.
4. Add the coconut oil to the bowl and use a fork or pastry cutter to combine until crumbly.
5. Sprinkle the crumble mixture over the peaches.

6. Bake for 25-30 minutes or until the topping is golden brown.

Vegan Chocolate Mousse

Ingredients:

- 1 can of chilled coconut cream
- 1/4 cup cocoa powder
- 1/4 cup maple syrup
- 1 tsp vanilla extract
- pinch of salt

Instructions:

1. Scoop the chilled coconut cream from the can into a mixing bowl.
2. Using an electric mixer, beat the coconut cream for 2-3 minutes until it becomes fluffy.
3. Add in the cocoa powder, maple syrup, vanilla extract, and salt.
4. Continue to beat the mixture until well combined and the mousse becomes thick and creamy.
5. Chill in the refrigerator for at least 30 minutes before serving.

Vegan Lemon Bars

Ingredients:

For the crust:

- 1 1/2 cups flour
- 1/2 cup vegan butter
- 1/4 cup powdered sugar

For the filling:

- 1 cup silken tofu
- 1/2 cup lemon juice
- 1/2 cup sugar
- 1/4 cup flour
- 1 tsp baking powder
- zest of 1 lemon

Instructions:

1. Preheat the oven to 350°F.
2. In a mixing bowl, combine the flour, vegan butter, and powdered sugar to make the crust.
3. Press the crust into a greased baking dish and bake for 20 minutes.
4. In another mixing bowl, combine the silken tofu, lemon juice, sugar, flour, baking powder, and lemon zest to make the filling.

5. Pour the filling over the crust and bake for another 20-25 minutes or until the filling is set.
6. Let cool before slicing into bars and serving.

Vegan Raspberry Cheesecake Bars

Ingredients:

- 1 cup almonds
- 1 cup dates, pitted
- 1 1/2 cups cashews, soaked overnight
- 1/3 cup coconut oil, melted
- 1/3 cup maple syrup
- 1/3 cup fresh raspberries
- 1 tsp vanilla extract
- juice of 1 lemon
- pinch of salt

Instructions:

1. In a food processor, pulse almonds and dates until crumbly.
2. Press the mixture into the bottom of an 8x8 inch baking dish lined with parchment paper.
3. In a blender, combine soaked cashews, melted coconut oil, maple syrup, raspberries, vanilla extract, lemon juice, and salt until smooth and creamy.

4. Pour the filling over the crust.
5. Freeze for at least 3 hours or until firm.
6. Cut into bars and serve chilled.

Vegan Lemon Poppy Seed Loaf

Ingredients:

- 1 1/2 cups all-purpose flour
- 1/2 cup almond flour
- 1 tsp baking powder
- 1/2 tsp baking soda
- 1/4 tsp salt
- 1/3 cup coconut oil, melted
- 3/4 cup sugar
- 1/2 cup unsweetened almond milk
- 1/4 cup fresh lemon juice
- 1 tbsp lemon zest
- 1 tbsp poppy seeds

Instructions:

1. Preheat oven to 350°F.
2. In a bowl, whisk together all-purpose flour, almond flour, baking powder, baking soda, and salt.

3. In another bowl, mix together melted coconut oil and sugar.
4. Stir in almond milk, lemon juice, lemon zest, and poppy seeds.
5. Add the dry ingredients to the wet mixture and mix until just combined.
6. Pour the batter into a greased loaf pan.
7. Bake for 40-45 minutes or until a toothpick inserted in the center comes out clean.
8. Let cool before serving.

Vegan Coconut Chocolate Truffles

Ingredients:

- 1/2 cup coconut cream
- 8 oz vegan dark chocolate, chopped
- 1/2 tsp vanilla extract
- 1/4 tsp salt
- 1/2 cup unsweetened shredded coconut

Instructions:

1. In a saucepan, heat coconut cream over medium heat until just simmering.
2. Remove from heat and add chopped chocolate, vanilla extract, and salt.

3. Stir until the chocolate is completely melted and smooth.
4. Chill the mixture in the refrigerator for 1-2 hours or until firm.
5. Roll tablespoon-sized balls of the mixture in shredded coconut.
6. Chill the truffles in the refrigerator for an additional 15 minutes before serving.

www.ingramcontent.com/pod-product-compliance
Lightning Source LLC
LaVergne TN
LVHW010344200726
843507LV00010B/1633